KNOW IT ALL
DINOSAURS

By Louise Nelson

BookLife PUBLISHING

©2022
BookLife Publishing Ltd.
King's Lynn, Norfolk
PE30 4LS, UK

All rights reserved.
Printed in Poland.

A catalogue record for this book is available from the British Library.

ISBN: 978-1-80155-614-9

Written by:
Louise Nelson

Edited by:
William Anthony

Designed by:
Dan Scase

All facts, statistics, web addresses and URLs in this book were verified as valid and accurate at time of writing. No responsibility for any changes to external websites or references can be accepted by either the author or publisher.

PHOTO CREDITS

All images are courtesy of Shutterstock.com. With thanks to Getty Images, Thinkstock Photo and iStockphoto.
Front cover: YuRi Photolife, josefauer, LuFeeTheBear, Natalia Gorbach, Hedzun Vasyl, Marques, Herschel Hoffmeyer, Vereshchagin Dmitry, Ton Bangkeaw, Barks, Mark Brandon 4&5 – Lotus_studio, metha1819, Hedzun Vasyl, kamomeen, Daniel Eskridge, Natalia Gorbach, MaryValery, Daniel Eskridge. 6&7 – Ton Bangkeaw, Marques, Herschel Hoffmeyer, solarseven. 8&9 – Puwadol Jaturawutthichai, Herschel Hoffmeyer, Vac1, David Herraez Calzada, Herschel Hoffmeyer, metha1819, Daniel Eskridge. 10&11 – Warpaint, Nobu Tamura, YuRi Photolife, Dotted Yeti, Elenarts, Digital Genetics, Warpaint, Vac1, Warpaint, Ton Bangkeaw, YuRi Photolife, DM7, Daniel Eskridge. 12&13 – Vac1, Matis75, Catmando, Warpaint. 14&15 – Royal Ontario Museum Eoraptor, Josep , Gelpi Curto. 16&17 – Herschel Hoffmeyer, Daniel Eskridge, Catmando, Elenarts. 18&19 – VaLiza, Herschel Hoffmeyer, Steve Bower. 20&21 – FunkMonk, Bodor Tivadar, Ton Bangkeaw, VaLiza Wlad74. 22&23 – Herschel Hoffmeyer, Warpaint, Ton Bangkeaw, YuRi Photolife, Durbed. 24&25 – DM7, Puwadol Jaturawutthichai, Vinicius Tupinamba, Puwadol Jaturawutthichai, Herschel Hoffmeyer. 26&27 – SergiyN, Daniel Eskridge, Filippo Vanzo, vadimserebrenikov, Catmando. 28&29 – Ton Bangkeaw, Alexander Pekour, AKKHARAT JARUSILAWONG, Danita Delimont, kamomeen, pets in frames. 30&31 – Limbitech. 32&33 – Dream Expander, metha1819, Olhastock, ixpert, kamomeen, YuRi Photolife, David Herraez Calzada, Vac1. 34&35 – New Africa, CHOKCHAI POOMICHAIYA, metha1819, Suwat wongkham, YuRi Photolife, Ton Bangkeaw, Vac1, YuRi Photolife. 36&37 – Betsart, Ton Bangkeaw, YuRi Photolife, marilyn barbone. Did You Know icon: Noch

CONTENTS

Page 4	**Dinosaurs**
Page 6	**Key Ideas**
Page 8	**What Are Dinosaurs?**
Page 10	**Timeline: Dinosaurs**
Page 12	**The Triassic Period**
Page 14	**Eoraptor**
Page 16	**The Jurassic Period**
Page 18	**Allosaurus**
Page 20	**Case Study: Sauropods**
Page 22	**The Cretaceous Period**
Page 24	**Tyrannosaurus Rex**
Page 26	**Parasaurolophus**
Page 28	**Ankylosaurus**
Page 30	**What Happened to the Dinosaurs?**
Page 32	**Believe It or Not!**
Page 34	**Activities**
Page 36	**Quick Quizzes**
Page 38	**Glossary**
Page 40	**Index**

**Words that look like this can be found in the glossary on page 38.
Key ideas you will need can be found on page 6.**

DINOSAURS

Once upon a time, before humans walked the Earth, there was the time of the dinosaurs. Since their discovery, these incredible **reptiles** have captured our imaginations. But how much do you really know about these ancient creatures?

Dinosaurs walked the Earth for millions of years, then all died out around 66 million years ago (MYA).

Were all dinosaurs big?

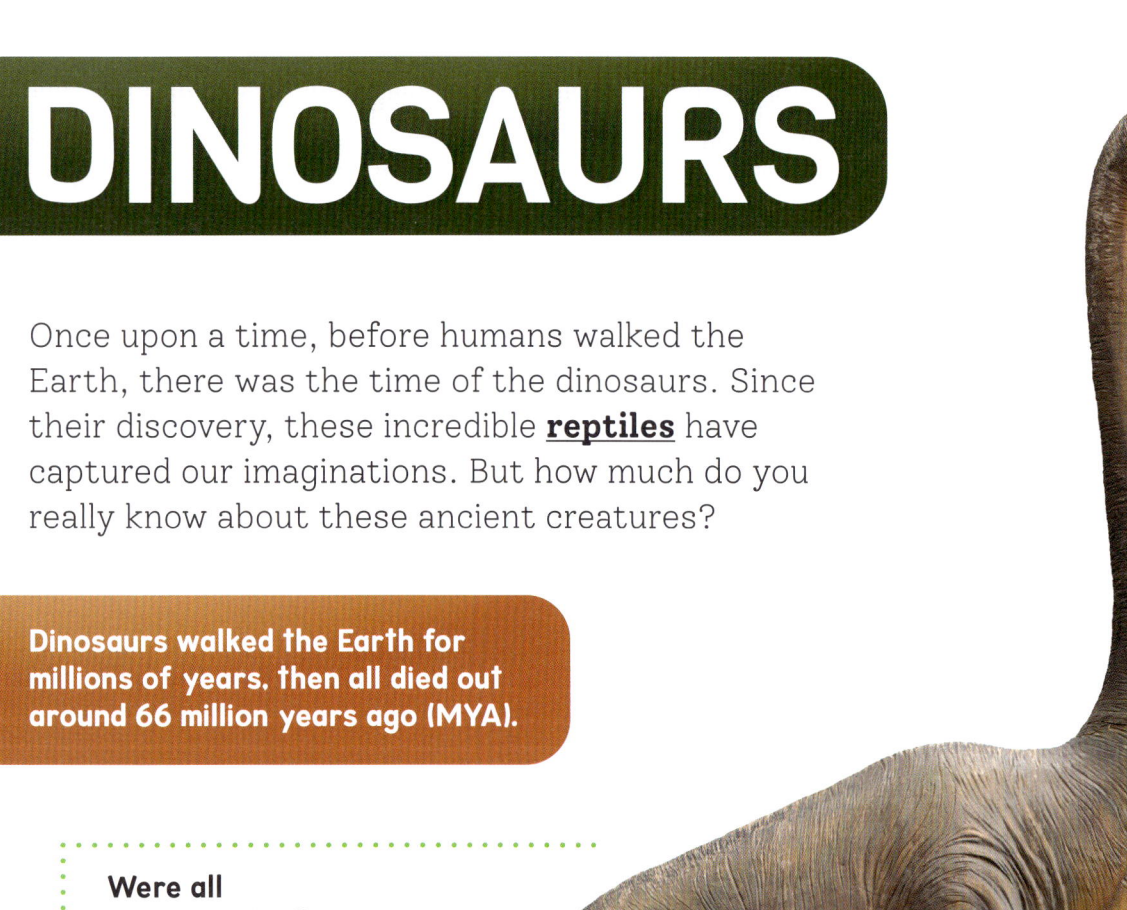

How long ago did dinosaurs live?

Were all dinosaurs this scary?

Where did they all go?

Many creatures that we think of as dinosaurs, such as plesiosaurus and pterodactyl, were not dinosaurs at all. They were a different type of reptile. Dinosaurs mostly lived on land.

DID YOU KNOW?

PTERODACTYL

PLESIOSAUR

We are still learning a lot about dinosaurs. For a long time, we thought dinosaurs were scaly and smooth, like modern crocodiles. Now, we know that many dinosaurs had feathers, like birds. In this book, we are going to look at what we know today, but who knows what we will discover in the future – there is still so much to find out!

People who look at dinosaur bones to find out about them are called palaeontologists. Palaeontologists also learn about other life that was around at that time, such as fish and **mammals**.

This is what palaeontologists in the early 1900s thought Diplodocus looked like.

Today, we think Diplodocus might have looked like this. Do you think we have finally got it right?

5

KEY IDEAS

Here are some key words and ideas you need to know when reading this book. Read them through before you start, then check back here if you need to remember.

CARNIVORES, HERBIVORES AND OMNIVORES

Animals that mostly eat meat are carnivores. Animals that mostly eat plants are herbivores. Animals that eat both plants and meat are omnivores.

Herbivores have flat teeth for grinding up plants.

Carnivores have sharp teeth for tearing up meat.

PREDATORS, PREY AND SCAVENGERS

Animals that hunt other animals for meat are called predators. The animals they hunt are called prey. Predators are all carnivores or omnivores. Prey animals can be carnivores, omnivores or herbivores.

Scavengers eat any meat they can find.

EXTINCTION EVENT

Life on Earth is always changing. Plants and animals have to **adapt** to these changes, such as changes in the **climate** or available food, if they are to survive. If animals cannot adapt quickly enough, then that type of animal can die out until there are none left. This is called extinction.

Occasionally, something so large happens to the planet that many types of animal become extinct all at once. Extinction events can happen because of massive volcanoes, **asteroid** collisions and dramatic changes in climate, such as a huge drought or an ice age.

WHAT ARE DINOSAURS?

Dinosaurs were a group of large reptiles. They lived from 245 MYA to around 66 MYA. The word 'dinosaur' means 'terrible lizard' in ancient Greek. There were lots of different types of dinosaur. Some were very small and some were very large.

BACKBONE

VERTEBRA

Dinosaurs were vertebrates. This means they had a backbone made up of smaller bones, called vertebrae.

Some dinosaurs walked on four legs..

.. and some walked on two legs.

We know about dinosaurs because we study their bones as <u>fossils</u>.

There were two types of dinosaur. These were bird-hipped dinosaurs and lizard-hipped dinosaurs.

Bird-hipped dinosaurs were often herbivores. Their hips were far back on their bodies, to make room for a large stomach and **intestines** needed for eating plant foods. This group includes Stegosaurus, Ankylosaurus and Triceratops.

TYRANNOSAURUS REX

Can you see the hips at the back of Stegosaurus, as well as its large belly?

Lizard-hipped dinosaurs had hips that were high and forwards on their bodies. This made them fast runners. These dinosaurs were mostly predators that needed to move quickly to catch their prey, but didn't eat lots of plant food. This group includes Tyrannosaurus rex.

STEGOSAURUS

The biggest dinosaurs were also lizard-hipped.

BRACHIOSAURUS

TIMELINE: DINOSAURS

TRIASSIC PERIOD: 252–201 MYA

EARLY
LYSTROSAURUS

LATE
EORAPTOR
HERRERASAURUS
ASYLOSAURUS

LATE
ANKYLOSAURUS
NIGERSAURUS
PSITTACOSAURUS

ARGENTINOSAURUS
PACHYRHINOSAURUS
TYRANNOSAURUS REX

THE TRIASSIC PERIOD

EARLY TRIASSIC

237 million years ago

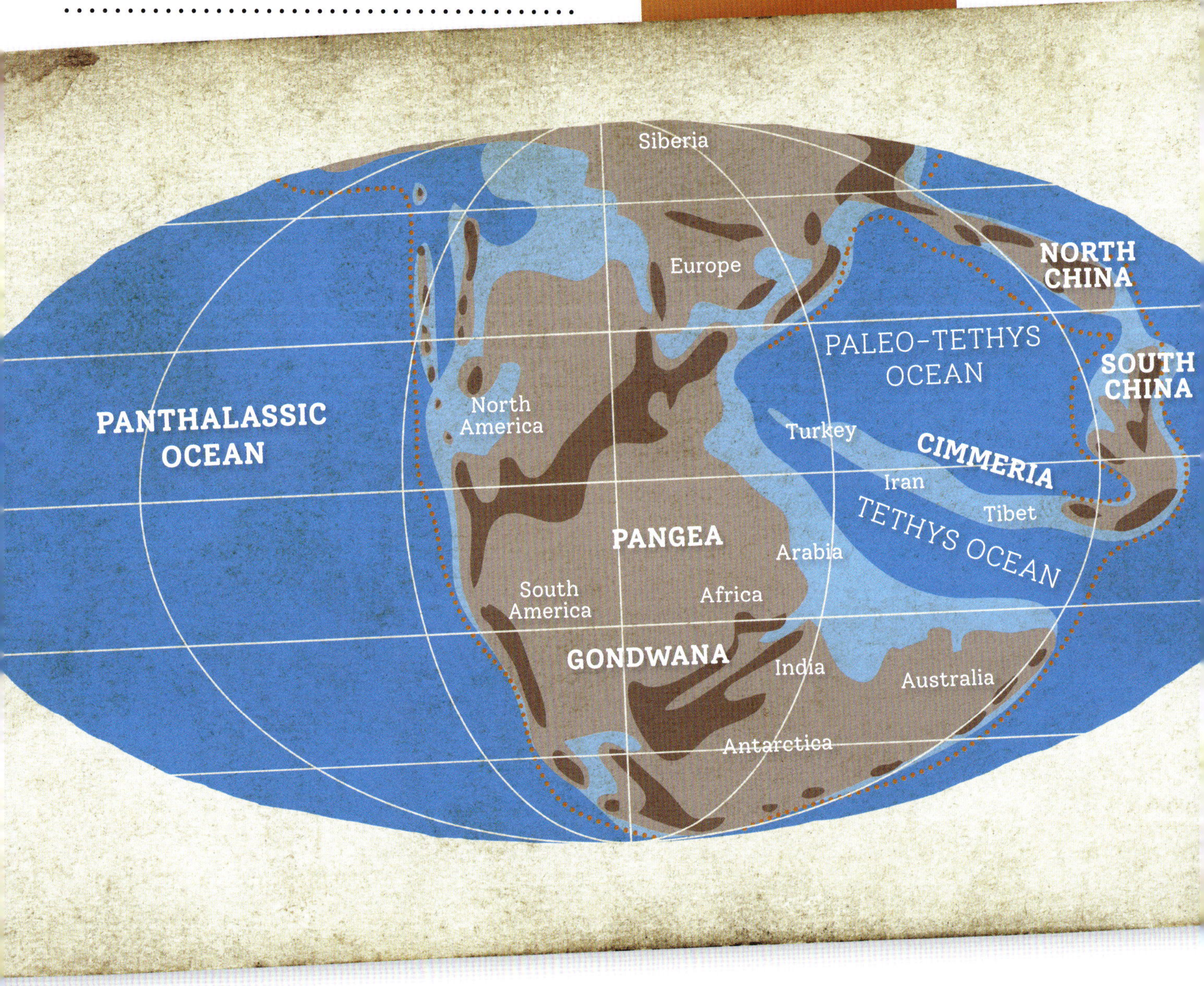

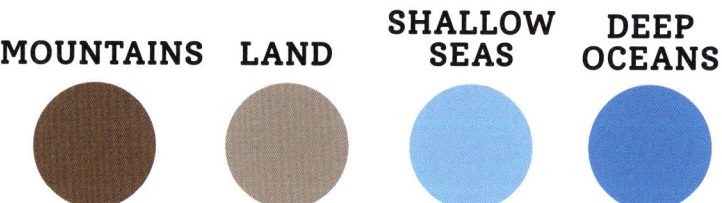

The earliest dinosaurs that we know of lived in the Triassic Period. This period of time lasted from 252–201 MYA. At this time, all the land on Earth was together and made up one **landmass**, called Pangea.

This map shows what Pangea would have looked like in the Triassic Period. The names of the modern **continents** tell you where these areas are now.

Pangea slowly split apart through the Mesozoic Era. When the last dinosaurs were wiped out, the continents looked almost exactly like they do today.

Coelophysis was a dinosaur of the Late Triassic. It was about the size of a large dog, with a long tail. It was a carnivore with small, sharp teeth.

Plateosaurus was a Triassic herbivore.

Herrerasaurus measured around three metres from nose to tail.

Triassic dinosaurs didn't rule the Earth like later dinosaurs. They had to share Pangea with other life forms, such as lizards, **amphibians**, insects and mammal-like reptiles.

The Triassic Period ended with an extinction event.

Lystrosaurus was a mammal-like reptile that lived in the early Triassic Period.

We are not sure what caused so many plants and animals to suddenly die out, but it is thought that volcanoes changed the climate.

EORAPTOR

One of the earliest dinosaurs we know about is Eoraptor. Eoraptor was rather small, not much bigger than a large cat. Eoraptor was a theropod. This type of dinosaur walked on two legs and ate meat.

128 cm

Sharp claws for hunting

Strong legs for running

Long tail helps balance

Early dinosaurs, such as Eoraptor, were not specialists. This means their bodies were not yet particularly good at any one skill. Instead, they were rather good at both hunting and running, but did not have the special **features** that make later dinosaurs VERY good at one thing.

Eoraptor lived around 228 MYA.

Eoraptor probably hunted mostly insects and small animals. It may have scavenged larger animals too.

This Panphagia would have made a good meal for an Eoraptor.

Pisanosaurus would have been easy prey for the bigger Eoraptor.

DID YOU KNOW?

Scientists are not sure whether Eoraptor had feathers or scales.

THE JURASSIC PERIOD

The extinction event at the end of the Triassic Period led to the Jurassic Period beginning. Dinosaurs had become more specialised, with new features on their bodies. Some herbivores developed strong armour or spikes for protection. Predators developed sharp eyesight and fierce claws.

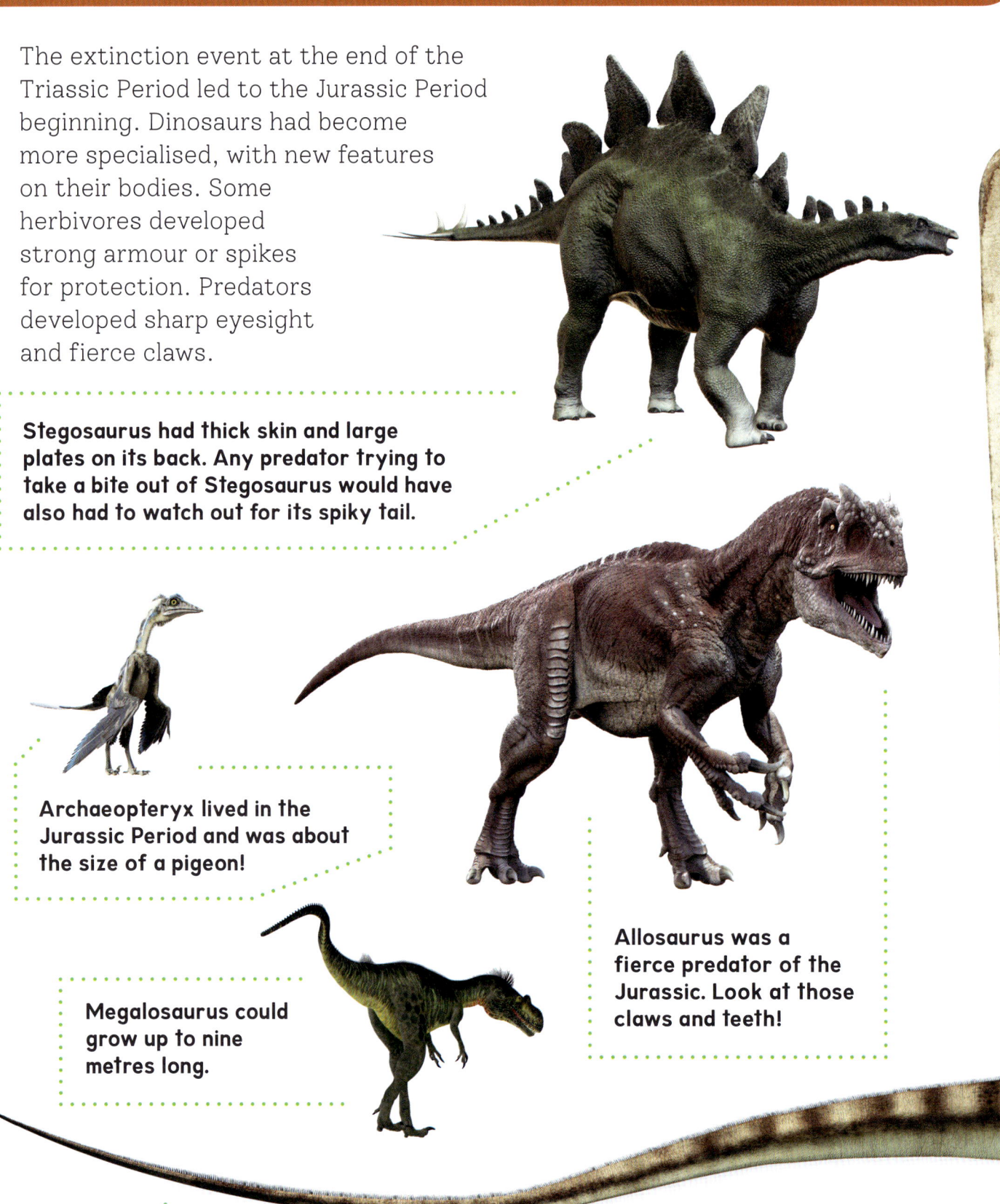

Stegosaurus had thick skin and large plates on its back. Any predator trying to take a bite out of Stegosaurus would have also had to watch out for its spiky tail.

Archaeopteryx lived in the Jurassic Period and was about the size of a pigeon!

Megalosaurus could grow up to nine metres long.

Allosaurus was a fierce predator of the Jurassic. Look at those claws and teeth!

Diplodocus was huge! Diplodocus could grow as long as two double-decker buses.

Because we have only found the hard parts of dinosaurs, such as bones and teeth, we do not know what colour they would have been.

The Jurassic Period lasted from 201 MYA to 145 MYA. During this time, the Earth's continents had begun to drift apart. The climate was changing and more plants began to appear.

LATE JURASSIC

152 million years ago

MOUNTAINS **LAND** **SHALLOW SEAS** **DEEP OCEANS**

Early dinosaurs of the Triassic had been small and shared similar features. In the Jurassic Period, all of that changed. As dinosaurs became more <u>diverse</u>, they came to rule the Earth...

ALLOSAURUS

Allosaurus was a large theropod dinosaur from the Jurassic Period. It was HUGE. Allosaurus could grow to 12 metres in length and weighed over two **tonnes**. Allosaurus was a specialist, built for hunting and eating meat.

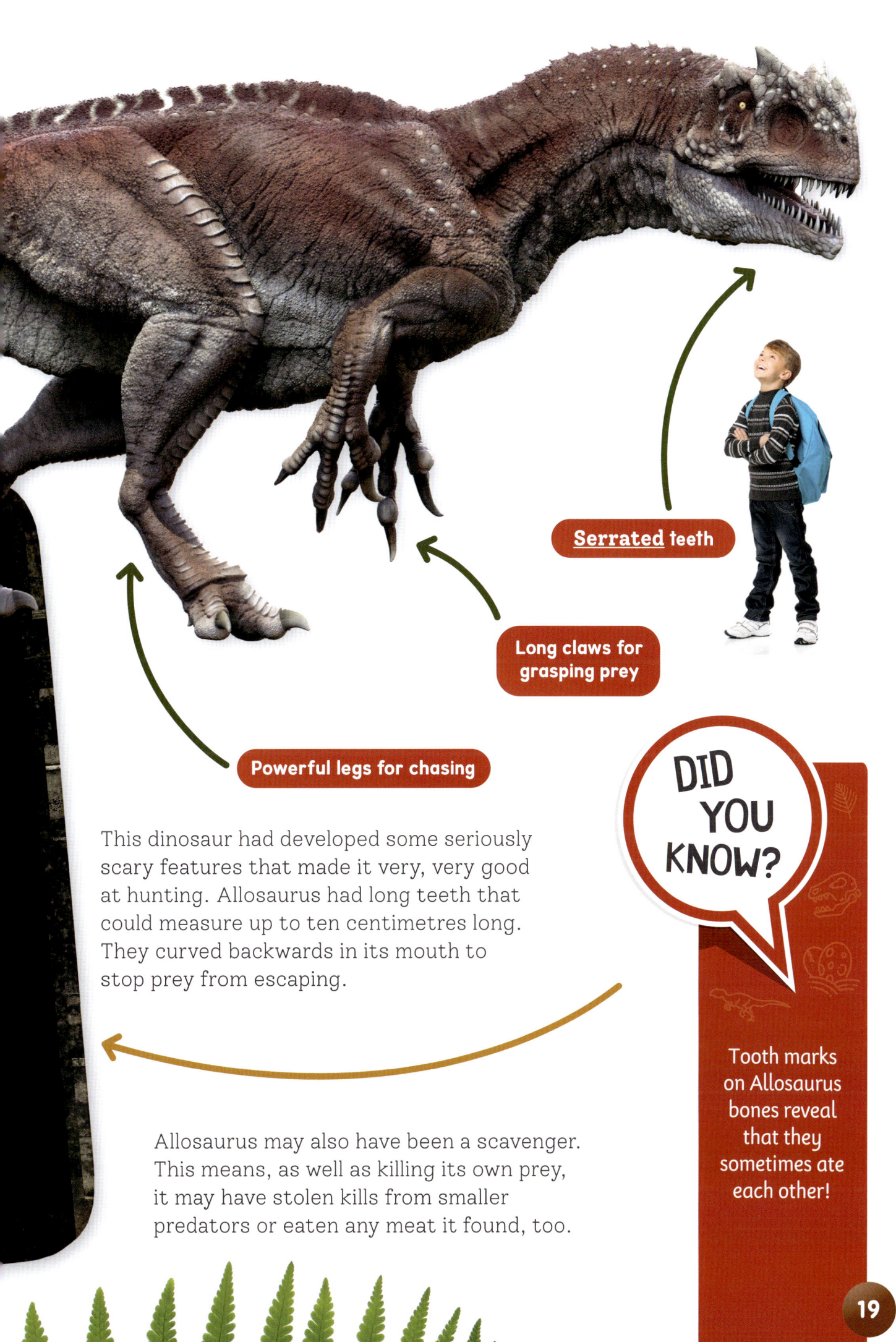

Serrated teeth

Long claws for grasping prey

Powerful legs for chasing

This dinosaur had developed some seriously scary features that made it very, very good at hunting. Allosaurus had long teeth that could measure up to ten centimetres long. They curved backwards in its mouth to stop prey from escaping.

Allosaurus may also have been a scavenger. This means, as well as killing its own prey, it may have stolen kills from smaller predators or eaten any meat it found, too.

DID YOU KNOW?

Tooth marks on Allosaurus bones reveal that they sometimes ate each other!

CASE STUDY: SAUROPODS

The sauropods became the biggest dinosaurs to ever walk the Earth. They were large herbivores with long necks and tails. They walked on four legs.

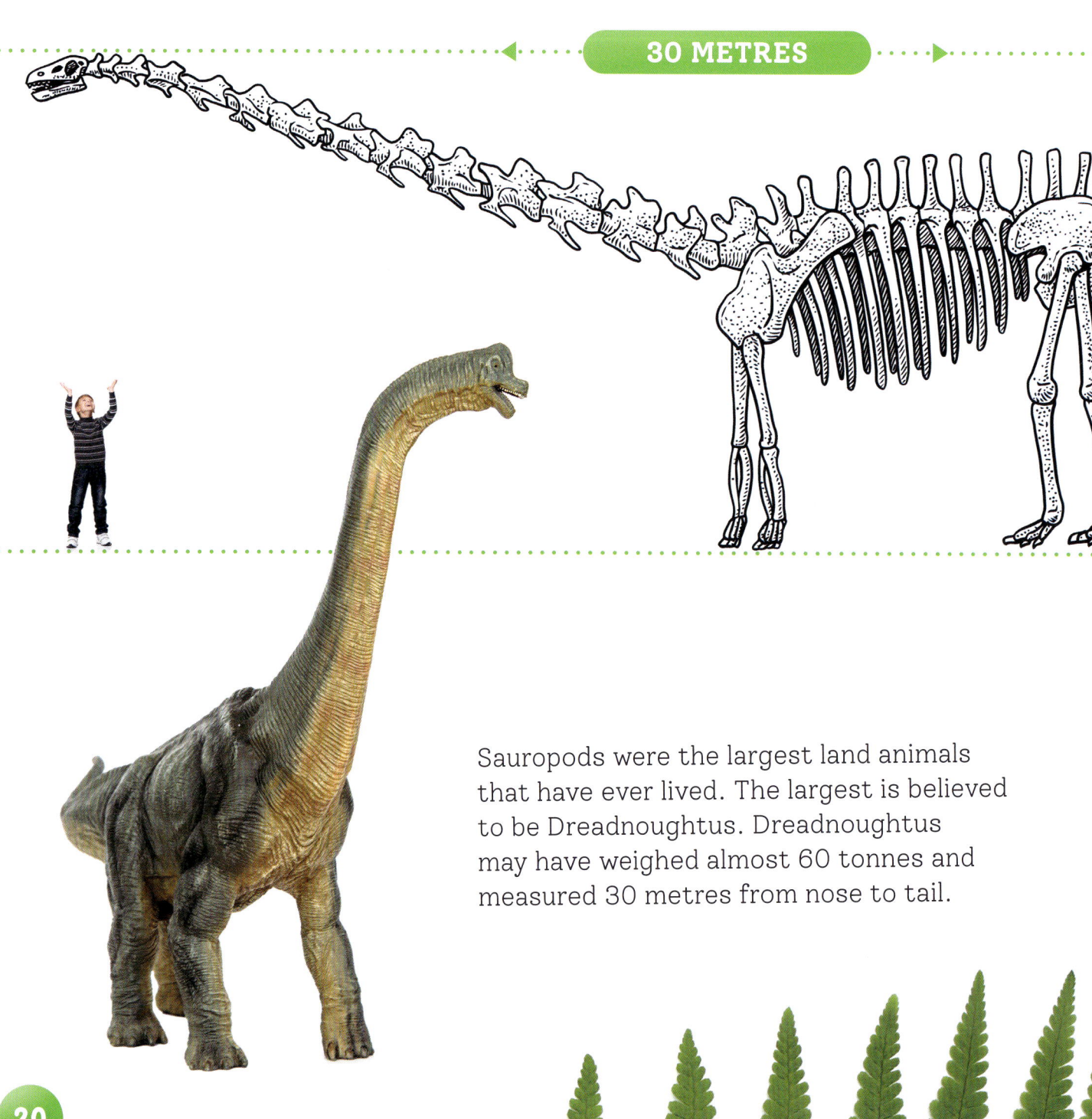

30 METRES

Sauropods were the largest land animals that have ever lived. The largest is believed to be Dreadnoughtus. Dreadnoughtus may have weighed almost 60 tonnes and measured 30 metres from nose to tail.

Sauropods first appeared in the early Jurassic Period, and quickly **evolved** to their largest sizes by the end of the period. Sauropods carried on into the Cretaceous Period.

BRACHIOSAURUS

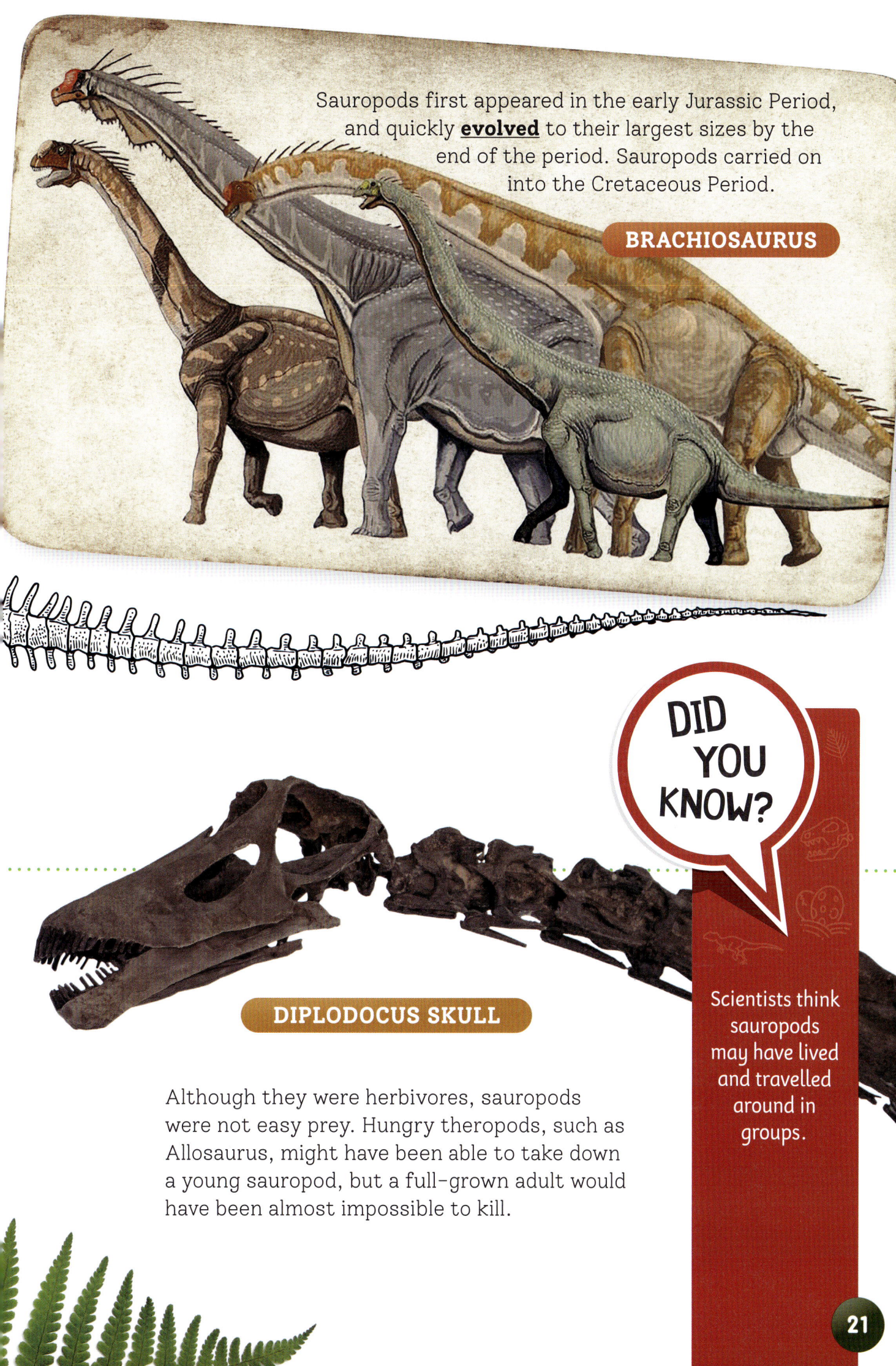

DIPLODOCUS SKULL

Although they were herbivores, sauropods were not easy prey. Hungry theropods, such as Allosaurus, might have been able to take down a young sauropod, but a full-grown adult would have been almost impossible to kill.

DID YOU KNOW?

Scientists think sauropods may have lived and travelled around in groups.

THE CRETACEOUS PERIOD

The Cretaceous Period began 145 MYA and ended 66 MYA. By this time, dinosaurs really did rule the land. Dinosaurs had become very specialised. A big range of features can be seen in the fearsome reptiles of the Cretaceous...

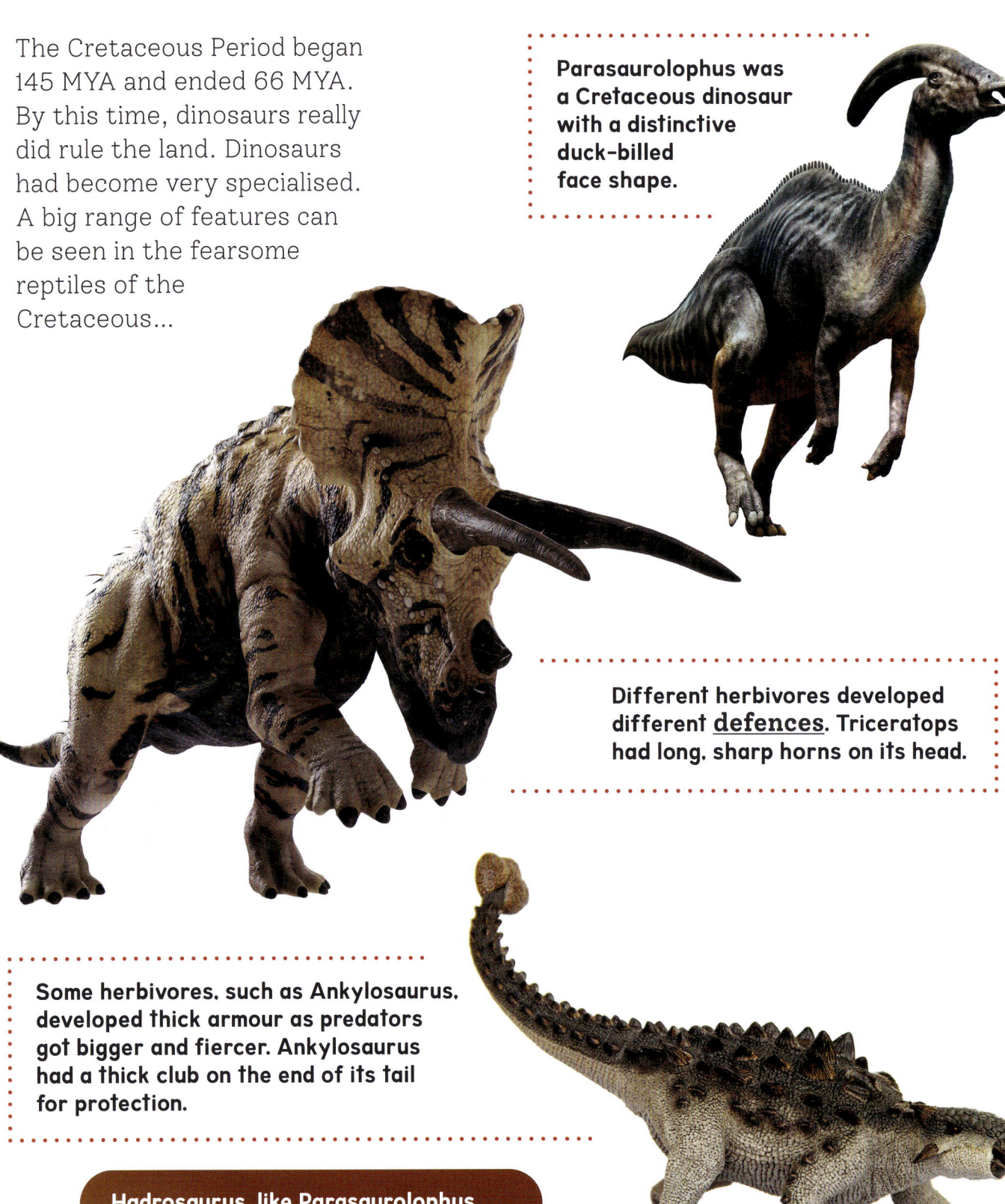

Parasaurolophus was a Cretaceous dinosaur with a distinctive duck-billed face shape.

Different herbivores developed different <u>defences</u>. Triceratops had long, sharp horns on its head.

Some herbivores, such as Ankylosaurus, developed thick armour as predators got bigger and fiercer. Ankylosaurus had a thick club on the end of its tail for protection.

Hadrosaurus, like Parasaurolophus, is thought to have lived in herds, much like large plant-eating animals today.

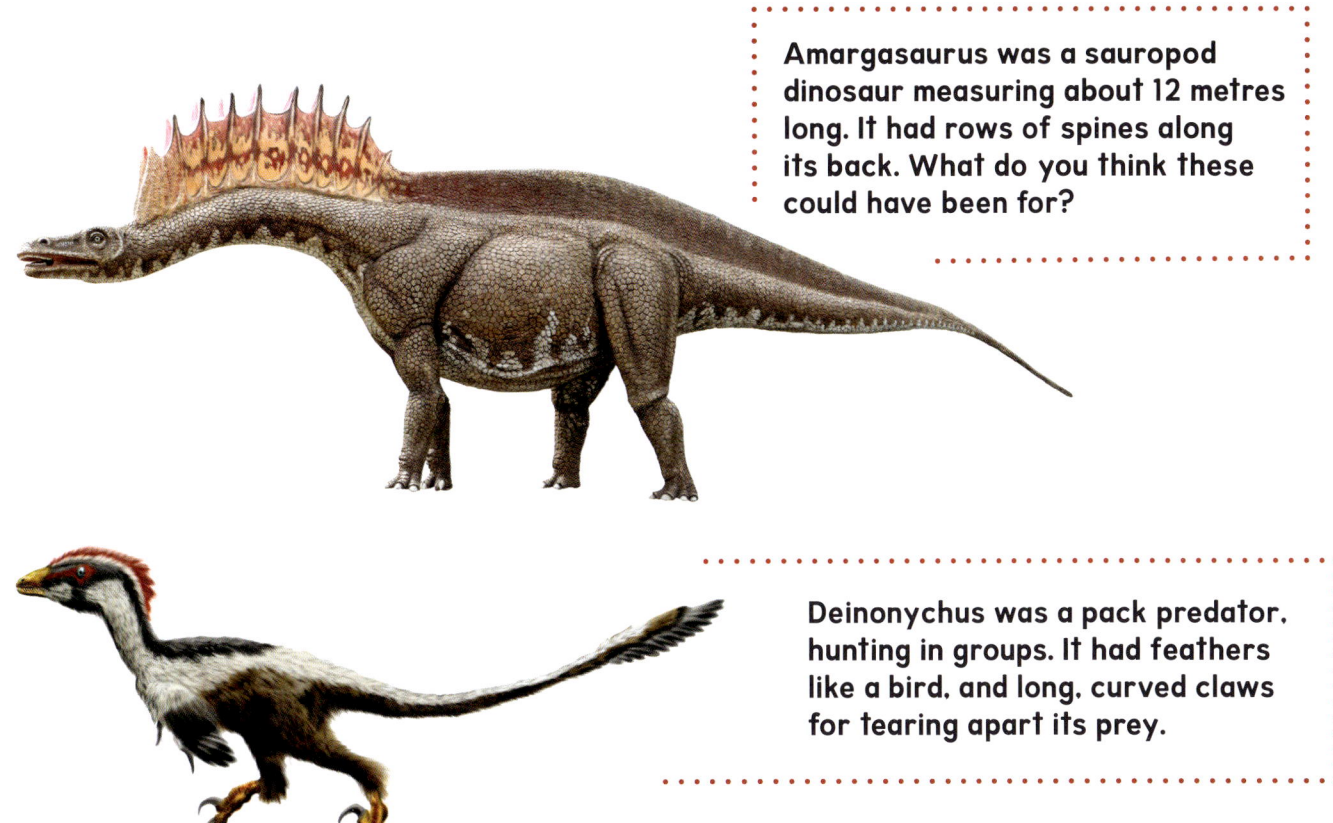

Amargasaurus was a sauropod dinosaur measuring about 12 metres long. It had rows of spines along its back. What do you think these could have been for?

Deinonychus was a pack predator, hunting in groups. It had feathers like a bird, and long, curved claws for tearing apart its prey.

By the end of the Cretaceous Period, the Earth's continents had moved into their current positions. Some of the best-known and most interesting dinosaurs come from this time.

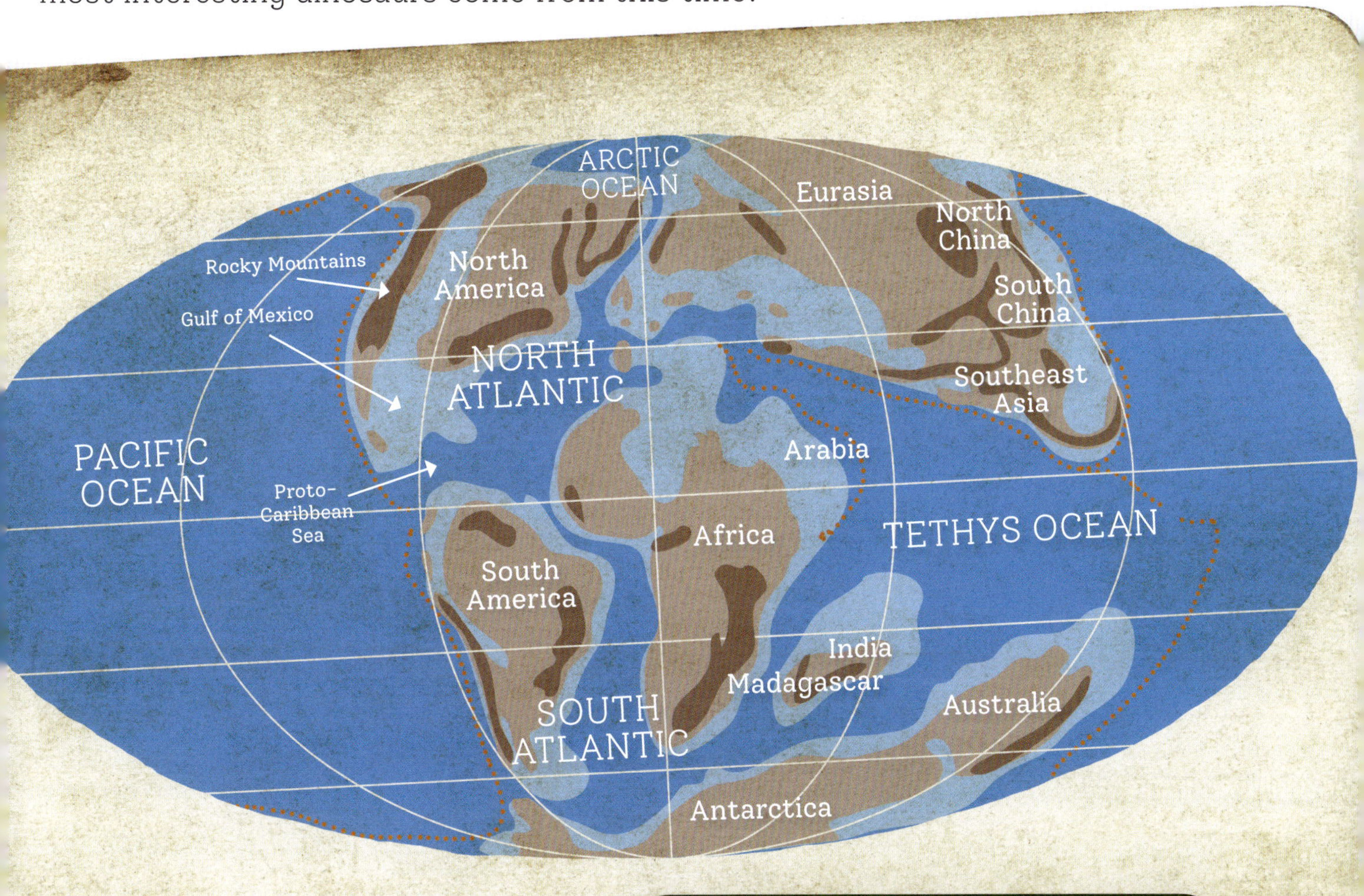

This map shows the new positions of the continents in the Cretaceous Period.

TYRANNOSAURUS REX

60 huge teeth that could crunch through bone

Huge head and jaws

Bite was three times stronger than a lion's

Powerful legs for running

DID YOU KNOW?

The largest T. rex fossil in the world can be seen in the US. Its nickname is Sue!

Amazing sense of smell

Tyrannosaurus rex. King of the dinosaurs. T. rex might be the most famous dinosaur predator, and for good reason. It was the biggest land predator that ever lived. T. rex could weigh up to seven tonnes and measure 12 metres from nose to tail.

Tyrannosaurus rex had eyes at the front of its head. This meant it could focus clearly on the prey in front of it. T. rex also had an amazing sense of smell, which helped it to **locate** prey from far away.

T. rex might have had a big bite, but it only had little arms.

PARASAUROLOPHUS

Parasaurolophus lived in the late Cretaceous Period. Parasaurolophus was a large herbivore. Its name means 'crested lizard' and it had a large, curved crest on its head. The crest may have been used to make a sound, like blowing a horn.

Bony crest shaped like a horn

Crest may have helped it stay cool

Could run away on strong back legs

Could walk on two or four legs

Like many modern herbivores, Parasaurolophus probably lived in a herd with others. This provides safety in numbers. The sounds from its crest could have been used to **communicate** with the rest of the herd.

To find out if the crest was for sound, a group of scientists made a model of one, and blew into it! It made a deep sound, like a modern **woodwind instrument**.

DID YOU KNOW?

In the 1930s, some scientists thought that Parasaurolophus' crest had a hole in it, which it used as a snorkel for breathing underwater! Now, we know this is not true because we know the crest did not have a hole in the end.

ANKYLOSAURUS

If the Cretaceous Period had the world's fiercest predators, it had some of the most creative defences too. Herbivores from this period had developed lots of ways to defend themselves, from spiky weapons to heavy armour.

Tail club may have been used for defence or attack

Heavy armour plates are hard to bite through

Big tummy is soft, but tucked underneath

Heavy skull

Ankylosaurus wasn't just tough – it was big. It could reach seven metres in length and weigh up to four tonnes. Both its hard head and heavy tail would have struck quite a blow. Its armour plates and spikes were made of heavy bone.

These bony plates are called scutes. Modern animals have scutes too, although they are not as heavy or thick.

Scutes on an alligator

The scutes on the shell of a tortoise are <u>fused</u>, just like Ankylosaurus. Ankylosaurus means 'fused lizard'.

WHAT HAPPENED TO THE DINOSAURS?

At the end of the Cretaceous Period, the dinosaurs disappeared in a massive extinction event. There have been lots of **theories** about what caused this, but now we think we know what happened. A large asteroid probably collided with the planet, causing a huge disaster that spread over the whole planet. The climate changed very quickly, and not even the dinosaurs were able to survive.

It is thought that the asteroid hit Earth in the shallow seas off the coast of Mexico. Huge fires and **tidal waves** would have followed. The Earth would have been surrounded with a huge cloud of dust and rock, and would have suddenly become dark and cold. Plants would have died without light, and the dinosaurs would have died soon after.

There are no more dinosaurs alive today – or are there? Turn the page to find out!

BELIEVE IT OR NOT!

Let's take a look at some amazing facts about dinosaurs.

Dinosaurs are the **ancestors** of today's birds. That's right! The T. rex is a distant relative of a chicken!

Dinosaurs walked the Earth for over 180 million years. That is a huge amount more time than humans have been around!

Dinosaur fossils have been found on every continent, including Antarctica.

Dinosaurs had babies by laying eggs. We know this because fossilised eggs have been found.

Triceratops had one of the biggest skulls of any land animal. Its skull could measure up to three metres long!

It is believed that people in ancient times may have discovered the fossils of dinosaurs and thought they were the bones of dragons or giants.

ACTIVITIES

Can you complete these fun activities?

Can you sort these dinosaurs into carnivores and herbivores? Remember that carnivores have weapons to attack with and many herbivores have defences, so look carefully at how specialised their bodies are.

a) TYRANNOSAURUS REX
b) STEGOSAURUS
c) BRACHIOSAURUS
d) VELOCIRAPTOR
e) SPINOSAURUS
f) PACHYCEPHALOSAURUS
g) UTAHRAPTOR

Answers: Carnivores: a, d, e, g. Herbivores: b, c, f

DESIGN-A-SAURUS

Think of all the features you've seen on dinosaurs. Now it's time to design your own ultimate dinosaur! Will you draw a fierce predator with the jaws of Tyrannosaurus rex, the curled claws of Velociraptor or the huge size of Spinosaurus? Or will your herbivore be the ultimate beast, covered in spikes, armour and huge, swinging weapons? Remember, we don't know what colour dinosaurs would have been, so maybe your dinosaur is **camouflaged** or has a flash of striking red and yellow? It's all up to you, so use your imagination!

QUICK QUIZZES

Can you beat our dino quizzes? 3... 2... 1... GO!

MEMORY TEST

Can you answer the questions? Check back through the book if you're not sure.

1. There are two types of dinosaur: lizard-hipped and which other?

2. What are the three periods the dinosaurs lived in called?

3. What was the name of the supercontinent made from all land on Earth in the Triassic Period?

4. Were sauropods herbivores or carnivores?

5. What defences did Ankylosaurus have?

POP!

Pop quiz question! What do we now think killed all the dinosaurs?

a) The land fell into the ocean

b) An asteroid hit the Earth

c) An illness that spread between the dinosaurs

Answer: b

Answers: 1. Bird-hipped 2. Triassic, Jurassic and Cretaceous 3. Pangea 4. Herbivores 5. Armour plates, spikes and a club tail

DINO-MAMA!

Help the mother find her eggs. Many dinosaurs were thought to be excellent parents that looked after their eggs and defended their babies while they were small.

GLOSSARY

A

adapt change over time to better suit an area or purpose

amphibians animals that can live both on land and in water

ancestors animals in the past from which modern animals developed

asteroid any one of thousands of rocky objects that circle around the Sun

C

camouflaged hidden by blending in with its surroundings

climate the usual weather in a certain place

communicate to pass information between two or more things

continents large areas of land, such as Africa or Europe, that are made up of many countries

D

defences things used for protection

diverse more wide-ranging and different

E

Era a section of time in history that often begins or ends with an important event

evolved changed and developed over time

F

features interesting or important parts of the body

fossils parts of plants and animals from a long time ago that have been kept in good condition inside rocks

fused joined together

I

intestines long tubes below the stomach that help to break down food

L

landmass a very large area of land

locate discover the exact position of something

M

mammals animals that have warm blood, have a backbone and produce milk to feed their children

P

periods sections of time in history

R

reptiles cold-blooded animals with scales that lay eggs to give birth

S

scavengers animals that feed on other animals which are already dead

serrated to have small notches like a saw that help to cut

T

theories explanations of how things work based on facts that have been tested

tidal waves very high, large waves in the ocean that are often caused by strong winds or an earthquake

tonnes a way of measuring how heavy something is, equal to 1,000 kilograms

W

woodwind instrument from a group of musical instruments that includes flutes, clarinets, oboes, bassoons and saxophones

INDEX

A

armour 16, 22, 28-29, 35

asteroids 7, 30-31, 36

C

carnivores 6-7, 13, 34, 36

claws 14, 16, 19, 23, 35

communication 27

continents 12, 17, 23, 32, 36

Cretaceous Period 11, 21-23, 26, 28, 30

crocodiles 5

D

defences 22, 28, 34, 36-37

dragons 33

E

eggs 33, 37

extinction events 7, 13, 16, 30

F

feathers 5, 15, 23

fossils 8, 24 32-33

H

herbivores 6-7, 9, 13, 16, 20-22, 26-28, 34-36

herds 22, 27

J

Jurassic Period 11, 13, 16-18, 21

M

Mesozoic Era 11-12

Mexico 17, 23, 31

O

omnivores 6-7

P

palaeontologists 5

Pangea 12-13

predators 7, 9, 16, 19, 22-23, 25, 28, 35

prey 7, 9, 15, 19, 21, 23, 25

S

sauropods 20-21, 23, 36

scavengers 7, 15, 19

spikes 16, 28-29, 35

T

teeth 6, 13, 16, 19, 24

theropods 14, 18, 21

Triassic Period 10-13, 16-17, 36

V

vertebrae 8